A Note to Parents and Teachers

DK READERS is a compelling program for beginning readers, designed in conjunction with leading literacy experts, including Dr. Linda Gambrell, director of the Eugene T. Moore School of Education, Clemson University, and past president of the National Reading Conference.

Beautiful illustrations and superb full-color photographs combine with engaging, easy-to-read stories to offer a fresh approach to each subject in the series. Each DK READER is guaranteed to capture a child's interest while developing his or her reading skills, general knowledge, and love of reading.

The four levels of DK READERS are aimed at different reading abilities, enabling you to choose the books that are exactly right for your children:

Level 1 – Beginning to read
Level 2 – Beginning to read
    alone
Level 3 – Reading alone
Level 4 – Proficient readers

The "normal" age at which a child begins to read can be anywhere from three to eight years old, so these levels are only a general guideline.

No matter which level you select, you can be sure that you are helping your child learn to read, then read to learn!

DK

LONDON, NEW YORK, MELBOURNE, MUNICH, AND DELHI

Senior Editor Beth Sutinis
Senior Art Editor Michelle Baxter
Publisher Chuck Lang
Creative Director Tina Vaughan
Production Chris Avgherinos
DTP Designer Milos Orlovic

Reading Consultant
Linda Gambrell, Ph.D.

Produced by
Shoreline Publishing Group LLC
Editorial Director James Buckley, Jr.
Art Director Tom Carling
Carling Design, Inc.

First American Edition, 2004

04 05 06 10 9 8 7 6 5 4 3
Published in the United States by DK Publishing, Inc.
375 Hudson St., New York, New York 10014

Published in Great Britain by Dorling Kindersley Limited.

ISBN: 0-7894-9896-0 (PB)
ISBN: 0-7894-9895-2 (HC)

A Catalog Record is available from the Library of Congress.

Color reproduction by Colourscan, Singapore
Printed and bound in Belgium by Proost

Photography credits:
(t: top; b: bottom)
AFP/Corbis: 17, 47; Bettmann/Corbis: 4b, 13, 14, 15, 18, 19, 34, 37;
Burstein Collection/Corbis: 21; Dean Conger/Corbis: 7;
Corbis: 33, 38, 39, 46; Corbis Sygma: 22, 27; DK Library: 32;
Scott Martin/Corbis: 16; NASA/Corbis: 24, 35,43;
PhotoEssentials: 6, 20, 23, 25, 26, 29, 30, 44, 45;
Rykoff Collection/Corbis: 8, 10; Reuters NewMedia/Corbis: 36;
Roger Ressmeyer/Corbis: 11, 41; Joseph Sohm/Corbis: 28;
Underwood & Underwood/Corbis: 4t, 5.

Discover more at
www.dk.com

Contents

DK READERS

SPACE HEROES:
AMAZING ASTRONAUTS
Written by James Buckley, Jr.

DK

What's out there?

Look! Up in the sky! Way, way, way up in the sky!

Earth is surrounded by the inky blackness of space. Since man first looked to the sky, he has wondered just what is out there.

Humans first tried many wild and dangerous ways to get off the ground and explore the skies. However, being shot out of a cannon did not get people very far.

The key to space

Enormous power is needed to break gravity, which keeps us on the Earth. American scientist Robert Goddard invented rockets, which make space travel possible.

Then, midway through the 20th century, rocket power gave humans the chance to explore space and find out just what is out there.

Huge rockets were built beginning in the 1950s in an effort to reach outer space. After years of tests, it was time to put a human being in a rocket. Only a person could tell the rest of the world about the joy and wonder of seeing Earth from space.

The astronauts chosen for this job would need to be brave, tough, and smart. No one knew what lay ahead of them. There would be danger, but also great adventure.

In 1961, we took the first steps on that trip when Alan Shepard became the first American in space.

Alan Shepard

Shepard is pulled from the water after his 15-minute flight. 7

Yuri Gagarin

The first creatures from Earth to rocket into space were not people: they were animals! A monkey named Gordo and a dog named Laika rode into space.

This postage stamp honors Soviet hero Yuri Gagarin.

The success of their flights inspired scientists to try to put a human into space. It was a race between the United States and the Soviet Union. Which country would launch the first human.

12
АПРЕЛЯ
1961

Who would that human be?

In the Soviet Union, a group of 20 pilots had received training to become cosmonauts (the Russian word for astronaut). Two men were finalists to make the first flight aboard a rocket called Vostok I. Who would it be?

Just days before the flight, an Army pilot was chosen. Yuri Gagarin would become the first person in space—if he could survive the flight.

He blasted off on April 12, 1961, just two weeks before Alan Shepard. The powerful rocket pressed Gagarin into his seat as it went zooming into orbit. He circled the Earth for 108 minutes. Huge parachutes guided his capsule safely back to Earth.

Gagarin instantly became a hero to his country and he received many honors. A crater on the moon and a city in Russia are named for Gagarin, the first person in space.

Yuri Gagarin

The Soviet Union

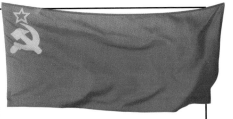

Until it was broken up into Russia and other countries in 1989, the Union of Soviet Socialist Republics (U.S.S.R.) battled the United States in the "space race." The largest part of the U.S.S.R. is known today as Russia.

John Glenn

Now that men had returned safely from space, more flights were planned. Brave astronauts were needed to take up the challenge of space flight.

In 1958, NASA (National Aeronautics and Space Administration) had started the Mercury program. This program selected a group of top pilots to train as astronauts. The new astronauts had to undergo a series of difficult tests. Only the best and bravest and most physically fit passed. The "Mercury 7" astronauts became America's first space heroes.

One of the Mercury 7 was a pilot in the U.S. Marine Corps. John Glenn had flown in combat during World War II and the Korean War. In 1957, he was the first pilot to fly across the U.S. faster than the speed of sound. His next big flight would be faster—much faster.

As Glenn prepared for his space flight in 1962, many questions remained. Would the rockets work? Would his capsule keep him safe in outer space?

John Glenn wore this special helmet and protective suit for his first trip into space.

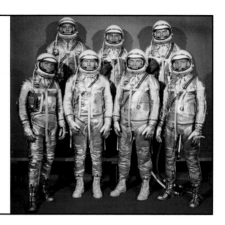

A team of heroes
NASA selected these seven astronauts to be in the first group to go to space. They were called the Mercury 7.

The big day arrived on February 20, 1962. As the countdown reached zero, the rocket blasted off, carrying its precious human cargo into space.

Glenn reached zero gravity quickly and steered his capsule into its orbital path. He zoomed around the Earth three times during his nearly five-hour flight. His capsule reached speeds of more than 17,000 miles per hour!

Upon his return from space as the first American to orbit the globe, Glenn became a national hero.

John Glenn's life of public service did not end when he landed on the Earth after his historic flight.

After working for NASA, he was elected to the U.S. Senate from Ohio in 1974.

Glenn was a senator for 24 years. Senator Glenn's expertise in aviation and space travel often came in handy when the Senate discussed space issues.

But even as he worked hard in Washington, D.C., Glenn dreamed of someday returning to outer space.

In October 1998, his dream came true. At 77, Senator Glenn became the oldest person ever to fly into space.

He spent nine days aboard the space shuttle Discovery. The first American to orbit the Earth had done it again!

Senator Glenn on his way to space . . . again!

Apollo astronauts

John Glenn and the Mercury astronauts had taken the first steps into outer space. A new group of American astronauts would soon take even bigger steps.

On May 25, 1961, President John F. Kennedy made a powerful statement. He said that America had a goal "of landing a man on the moon and returning him safely" before the end of the decade. That was less than nine years away and there were many obstacles to overcome.

NASA got right to work choosing astronauts.

President John Kennedy

Astronaut Scott Carpenter talks to the President.

The next group of astronauts were called Apollo astronauts. They began training immediately at bases in Florida and Texas. Each night these space pioneers would look up at the sky and see their goal: the moon.

The Saturn 5 rocket blasted Apollo astronauts into space.

The first challenge facing NASA was how to get the astronauts safely into space and to the moon. The moon is about 240,000 miles (385,000 km) from earth. Powerful rockets are needed to break Earth's gravity and carry capsules containing astronauts. The solution was the mighty Saturn 5 rocket.

The astronauts' capsules needed to be places where astronauts could work, eat, and even sleep. The voyage to the moon—and back—might take as long as 12 days!

Who was Apollo?

The Apollo space program was named after an ancient Greek god. Apollo was the god of the arts and culture. The Mercury program was named for the messenger of the Roman gods.

After some test flights of the Saturn rocket in 1966 and 1967, the Apollo missions got underway. Different teams of astronauts rode the mighty Apollo rocket while blasting off into space.

Though people had been flying into space for almost ten years, each flight was full of danger. New space suits were created to help guard astronauts from the dangers of space flight.

Neil Armstrong, Michael Collins, and Buzz Aldrin in their space suits.

Still, all the Apollo astronauts knew the risks. But they kept up their training. Next up were more test flights.

Apollo 8 orbited the moon for the

Edwin Aldrin on the moon.

first time in 1968. Apollo 9 tested the special craft that would be used on the moon itself. Apollo 10 made some final tests in May of 1969. NASA gathered this information and made the decision to try a moon landing. The crew of Apollo 11 was ready to make history.

On July 16, 1969, a Saturn 5 rocket carrying the three-man Apollo 11 crew lifted off in a roar of fire and smoke.

Four days later, millions of people around the world watched nervously as the crew reached orbit around the moon. Astronauts Neil Armstrong and Buzz Aldrin entered the special lunar craft, which was called "Eagle."

Slowly, Eagle dropped toward the moon's surface. Armstrong guided the craft carefully to a safe landing.

"The Eagle has landed!" he said.

After the two astronauts put on their special space suits and breathing packs, they were ready to leave Eagle.

Armstrong went first. As he stepped off the ladder, he became the first person ever to step on the moon. President Kennedy's goal had been reached by an American astronaut.

Man's footprints will remain forever on the lunar surface.

America's brave astronauts did not stop there. Over the next three years, five more Apollo missions took astronauts to the moon. They conducted many experiments and learned much about our closest neighbor in space.

The crew of Apollo 17 even got the chance to do a little driving in space. The lunar rover was a special car created for use on the moon so astronauts could explore further.

Astronauts drove this "lunar rover" on the moon.

From Apollo 11 to now, astronauts are treated as heroes.

Apollo 17 was the final mission to the moon. No one has returned there since Apollo astronauts Gene Cernan and Harrison Schmitt left the lunar surface on December 15, 1972.

One goal had been achieved, but many other space challenges lay ahead.

Space shuttle

Nearly 10 years after the final Apollo mission, NASA started the next wave of space flights. Instead of a rocket, however, astronauts would ride to the heavens in a new craft: the space shuttle.

Older rockets could not be reused and were expensive. The space shuttle was designed to be used many times. Even the rockets that shot it into orbit could be reused. Recycling had hit the space program!

Ocean explorer

The first space shuttle was named Columbia, after explorer Christopher Columbus. He crossed the Atlantic Ocean to land in the Americas in 1492.

Three huge fuel tanks power the space shuttle's rocket engines.   29

The space shuttle is one of the most amazing things that human beings have ever built. Scientists had to create a craft that would survive the pressure and vibrations of a rocket launch. But the craft also had to fly like a glider as it came in for a landing.

The shuttle looks like a large passenger airplane. Crew quarters and pilot seating are at the front of the plane. The main body of the shuttle is a huge cargo bay. Astronauts can release satellites and other craft into orbit from there.

Though the shuttle uses rockets to leave the Earth, it has no power of its own. To land, the pilot guides it through the sky before landing on rubber tires. The shuttle is going so fast when it lands it shoots out a huge parachute to help it stop.

For astronauts, the shuttle was the best ride in space!

Brave and bold

The new space shuttle would call for a new kind of astronaut. All the Apollo and Mercury astronauts were pilots first and astronauts second. Shuttle crew members might not be pilots at all!

MAX 100 KG

SPACE SIMULATOR

All astronauts go through months of training to learn how to survive in zero gravity.

Astronaut Robert Gibson looks over the shuttle controls.

The shuttle mission commanders and pilots, of course, were expert fliers. They knew how the complicated shuttle systems worked. In case of a problem, they could take over from the computers that helped run the shuttle.

Experienced space travelers would be part of any shuttle mission. However, NASA had plans to bring even more people into the space program.

The crew of the first shuttle mission prepares to take off.

To command the first shuttle mission aboard Columbia, NASA chose Apollo veteran John Young. He and copilot Bob Crippen would sit atop the most powerful machine ever built. The Columbia's rockets put out more power than 35 jumbo jets at takeoff.

On April 12, 1981, those huge rockets fired, carrying Columbia aloft.

Young and Crippen orbited the earth for two days aboard the shuttle before making a perfect landing in California. The shuttle was a huge success and a new age of space flight had begun.

The shuttle's huge cargo bay has room for a satellite!

Now that NASA knew the space shuttle would work, the agency began to expand the group of astronauts.

Since the first space flights, only women from the Soviet Union had gone into space. That changed with the shuttle. In 1983, Sally Ride became America's first female astronaut.

Female astronauts have become part of shuttle crews.

Space pioneer
Valentina Tereshkova became the first woman in space in 1963. She was a cosmonaut from the Soviet Union.

In the years since, more than 35 women have taken part in shuttle flights. They have been scientists, pilots, doctors, and space experts.

Both male and female astronauts act as shuttle "mission specialists." These astronauts do not fly the shuttle. Instead, they perform scientific experiments or work with satellites.

Each mission specialist has a specific job and trains for many months to learn to do their job in the zero gravity of outer space.

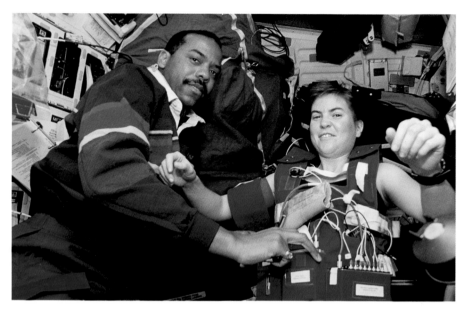

Dr. Bernard Harris checks a fellow astronaut in 1995.

All the Apollo and Mercury astronauts were white men. Shuttle crews, however, reflect the diversity of America. Members of many different ethnic groups have joined the shuttle program, training as pilots, commanders, and mission specialists.

In 1983, Air Force Colonel Guion Bluford became the first African-American in space.

In 1986, Franklin Chang-Díaz, a native of Costa Rica, became the first Hispanic-American in space. Chang-Díaz went on to set a record for taking part in the most shuttle flights. He flew on seven different shuttle missions.

Chang-Díaz studied to become an an engineer. Instead of building things, he used his scientific knowledge to help send satellites into orbit.

Franklin Chang-Díaz (left) waits to board the shuttle.

In the early years of space flights, the United States and the Soviet Union had all the astronauts. Now that the "space race" between those nations is over, today's astronauts come from many different countries.

Male and female astronauts from other nations have acted as mission specialists on space shuttle flights. They come from countries such as Germany, Japan, Brazil, Saudi Arabia, and India. Even cosmonauts from Russia, part of the old Soviet Union, have flown on space shuttle flights.

The whole world is filled with many types of people. So it makes sense that men and women of all sorts and from all places should be part of these amazing shuttle flights.

German astronaut Ulrich Walter floats in zero gravity.

Life in space

Whoever they are and wherever they are from, today's astronauts continue to experience remarkable adventures.

While they work in space, they live, eat, and sleep in zero gravity. They must learn to literally float through their day.

Some astronauts are trained to work outside the shuttle. The "space walks" they take are among the most dramatic events in an astronaut's life. They climb out of the safety of the shuttle into the darkness of space. Sometimes they are tied to the shuttle by strong cords. Other times they use a special rocket-powered backpack to get around.

Though they are hard at work, none of them can help but marvel at the spinning blue Earth below them.

Unlike earlier astronauts, today's space men and women do not have to come right home, either. Thanks to "space stations," astronauts can spend many months orbiting the Earth. They become space "citizens."

Space stations get energy from the sun using solar panels.

The Soviet Union built the first space stations in the 1970s. Salyut 6 lasted the longest, staying in orbit for almost six years. Cosmonauts flew to the station and stayed there for months, learning about life in space. In 1986, a station called Mir [Meer] was launched.

Mir was occupied until 1999 by astronauts from several countries, including the United States. Some visitors stayed for six months.

Recent shuttle flights have helped start construction of the International Space Station. The massive craft is being created by a team from more than a dozen countries.

From our first steps into space in the 1950s, human beings have come a long way.

Astronauts on space walks help build the space station.

Challenger's Christa McAuliffe is third from the left.

In honor . . .

An astronaut's job can be exciting. But astronauts also know their jobs can be very dangerous.

Two times, space shuttle crews have not returned from their missions into space. These tragic accidents took the lives of 14 astronauts.

In 1986, Challenger exploded shortly after takeoff. Schoolteacher Christa McAuliffe was part of the crew.

In 2003, Columbia broke up as it was coming in for a landing. Today's space travelers honor these heroes. The journey to space goes on.

Columbia crew members came from India, Israel, and the United States.

Glossary

aeronautics
The study of aircraft and flight.

aloft
In the air, above the ground.

aviation
Having to do with flight, especially flight powered by engines.

barrier
Something that blocks the path of something else.

boosters
Large rockets that join with a spacecraft's main rockets to help it escape gravity.

capsule
A small spacecraft in which astronauts travel while in space.

cargo bay
The large, open area in the back of the space shuttle from which satellites are launched or "deployed."

cosmonaut
The term used for an astronaut who comes from Russia or the Soviet Union.

countdown
The second-by-second count that NASA goes through before a launch.

crater
A huge, usually circular ditch or hole in the ground caused by the impact of a meteor (flying space rock).

deploy
Release or let go.

glider
A flying machine that does not have a motor and relies on wind currents to stay in the air.

gravity
The force that pulls things toward the ground and holds them there.

lunar
Having to do with the moon.

orbit
The journey around a planet or other body in space, such as the Earth or the moon.

orbital path
The route of a spacecraft or object as it spins around something else.

veteran
A person who has long experience in a particular field.

zero gravity
Lack of weight in space which allows objects to float around.